FIRE AND BRIMSTONE

by

Victor T. C. Smith

**Military Historian and Past President
The Brimstone Hill Fortress National Park Society**

The story of the Brimstone Hill Fortress, St. Kitts, West Indies. 1690-1853

First published 1992

Published by The Creole Publishing Company, Box 83, St. Kitts, West Indies
on behalf of The Brimstone Hill Fortress National Park Society and
funded by a grant from the British Development Division, Barbados.

CATALOGUE DATA
   Author:
      Smith, Victor T. C.
   Title:
      Fire and Brimstone
   Subject:
      St. Kitts' Brimstone Hill Fortress
      History & Description - Travel - Guide Books
   Publisher:
      The Creole Publishing Company, St. Kitts, West Indies.

ISBN   **0-944185-02-9**

Cover Picture by Frank Sharman • © 1991 Creole Graphics
Author's Picture by Philip Bayldon • © 1991 Victor T.C. Smith

Printed in Georgia, USA by Creole Graphics/Perfect Image

CONTENTS

INDEX OF ILLUSTRATIONS

FOREWORD

I consider it both a privilege and honour to have been asked by Victor Smith to write a Foreword for his history of the Brimstone Hill Fortress, which he has aptly named "Fire and Brimstone".

Victor has visited St. Kitts three times in recent years. His first visit in 1986 was arranged by the late His Excellency, Dr. Claudius Thomas, C.M.G., then High Commissioner in London for various Eastern Caribbean countries. The object of the trip which included St. Kitts, Nevis and St. Lucia was to give him an opportunity to consider and advise on the possibilities of developing certain forts on the islands as adjuncts to an ever increasing tourist trade.

He spent only three days on St. Kitts, but this proved to be a long enough time to arouse his great interest in Brimstone Hill, and he left here with the intention to return as soon as possible, in order to continue his work.

Not too long after this, he wrote that he saw a "window of opportunity" opening for Brimstone Hill and duly proceeded to arrange a second visit.

This second visit was achieved with a good deal of personal sacrifice to himself. He actually took leave without pay from his post as a British Civil Servant, to enable him to spend several weeks in St. Kitts and to do the necessary research in London on his return. British Executive Service Overseas again approved the cost of his return passage and the Brimstone Hill Society was pleased to provide financial assistance towards his local expenses.

Following his second visit, he completed a report on Brimstone Hill, which he recommends reading with a Feasibility Study by Frederick C. Gjessing, a highly experienced architect and restorer of historic buildings who resides in St. Thomas, U.S.V.I. This Feasibility Study for the development of the Brimstone Hill Fortress which had been commissioned for the Society by one of its members, is highly regarded by Victor.

The Brimstone Hill Society was able to interest officials of the British Development Division in the Caribbean, in Victor's work at Brimstone Hill. As a result the Division, together with the Head of his Civil Service Department in London, arranged for him to be seconded to St. Kitts in order to continue his work on the fortress.

Victor Smith has great experience as a researcher, as an historian, as an interpreter of the buildings and ruins of British forts and as an archaeologist. All of these skills have been generously utilised by him in his examination and reporting on Brimstone Hill. He has so far had three excellent articles on the fortress accepted for publication in well known historical journals.

Mention should also be made of the great physical efforts that he has put into his investigations of the Fortress area. For example, he has walked around the grounds surrounding the Hill on at least two occasions to locate the positions taken up by the French artillery during the siege of 1782. He has, of course, also analysed the locations of the British guns employed in 1782 in defending the Hill and of the relocation of many of the batteries and the addition of new cannon when the Fortress was reconstructed between 1783 and 1850.

Victor was of great assistance to the Society during preparations for the Tercentenary of the first arming with cannon of Brimstone Hill, on the 30th June 1690. He agreed to act as President of the Society, which post was then vacant, and here again brought to bear his wide experience in many other fields.

An ambitious programme had been prepared for the Tercentenary celebration of the first placement of cannon by the British on Brimstone Hill. The President of the Society had to be involved in a great deal of liaison work with Government officials, other helpers and participants in the programme. Victor represented the Society with his customary aplomb and ensured a successful commemoration.

This book is just another example of Victor Smith's commitment to Brimstone Hill. It will, I am sure, go a long way towards making the Fortress more widely known and better understood.

D. L. Matheson C.B.E.
President Emeritus
Brimstone Hill Fortress National Park Society

INTRODUCTION TO THE BRIMSTONE HILL FORTRESS

The Prince of Wales Bastion, Brimstone Hill Fortress
Sketch by Kevin Tatem

The Brimstone Hill Fortress is one of the most magnificent in the West Indies. It is also a reminder in stone and mortar of the often violent competition between England and France in historical times for control of the economic resources of the Eastern Caribbean.

From the seventeenth century until the Napoleonic wars, the two powers vied with each other for possession of the West Indian islands from which sugar, coffee and cotton could be cultivated for sale at high prices to meet consumer demand in Europe. The income thus derived not only benefited the merchant investors but was also used by the two powers to help finance their wars against each other.

To keep control of their resources in the West Indies required both England and France to maintain warships as best they could, to try to command the Caribbean Sea, backed by soldiers and fortifications on land.

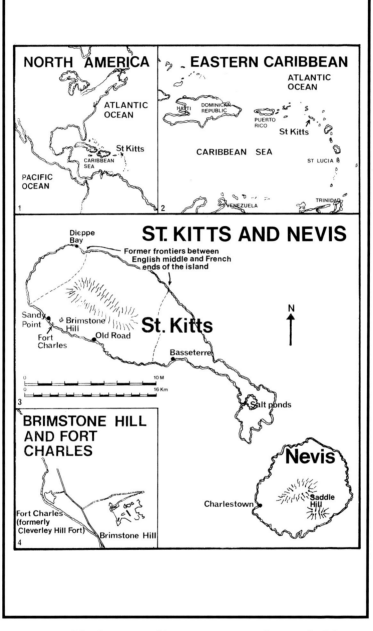

Maps of the location of St. Kitts, West Indies and of the Brimstone Hill Fortress.   V.T.C. Smith • 1991

Brimstone Hill was the most important of a number of English fortifications built on St. Kitts, whose main worth was the high value of its top quality sugar, extracted from the sugar cane which was profusely grown on the island.

From the inception of the Fortress, in the 1690's, until well into the nineteenth century, slaves toiled in building its walls whilst the soldiers lived and often died there. From its modest and tentative beginnings, the defences were developed into one of the most powerful and formidable fortresses in the Caribbean. It covered over 40 acres and was built on three levels, from the lowest at 550 feet to the highest at 780 feet.

All its works were carefully adapted to the form of the Hill and made the maximum use of the defensive possibilities offered by the terrain. By the early nineteenth century it came to be known as the "Gibraltar of the West Indies", not only because of its great strength but because from some angles the Hill looks a little like the Rock of Gibraltar.

The Hill saw action on no fewer than three occasions as will be described in this book: in 1690, 1782 and in 1806.

The Fortress is now being restored and presented to the visitor as a major defence heritage monument by the Brimstone Hill Fortress National Park Society.

Such is the historical importance of the Brimstone Hill Fortress, that an application has been made for its inclusion in the UNESCO World Heritage List.

CHAPTER ONE

THE HISTORY OF THE FORTRESS
Geology and Origins

The main geological feature of St. Kitts is the mountainous ridge, of volcanic origin, which runs down the centre of the island. Brimstone Hill, a prominent and striking feature of the landscape, is actually isolated from that ridge. It is not, as might be supposed from its appearance, an old volcano: it is, however, an upthrust of igneous rock, produced as a result of underlying volcanic forces in geological times. Its main structure is a grey stone called andesite. In places this has a covering of coral limestone, thus proving that the material which makes up the Hill was once below the surface of the sea. The name of the Hill is said to derive from the odour of sulphur which is released from a volcanic vent in the sea bed, a short distance from the nearby shore.

Little is known of the Hill before the joint settlement of St. Kitts by the English (in 1623) and by the French (in 1624). It is at least possible that, because of its distinctive shape, the original Amerindian inhabitants of the island assigned it some form of religious significance.

Brimstone Hill from the South. Photo by Victor T.C. Smith

The joint occupation of the island became a source of friction, division and strife between the English and the French. On the formal partitioning of St. Kitts between the two colonising peoples in 1627, the Hill came to be in the central, English part of the island. Initially, there was an agreement between the English and the French to share the valuable limestone deposits of the Hill. However, the English gradually began to see the limestone as exclusively their own property.

The strategic value of Brimstone Hill was not recognised until 1690. In that year the Hill echoed to the sound of guns mounted upon it for the first time. During the War of the Grand Alliance, the French had succeeded in capturing and holding the nearby English Fort Charles built on the shore below. The English managed to mount guns on the side of the Hill within range of the fort and a furious cannonade, linked with bombardment from the sea, forced the French to surrender. The dragging of guns up the steep slopes of the Hill had been difficult but had been successfully accomplished with the expertise of Governor Codrington's "Trusty Regiment of Sailors", an event commemorated in a special issue of postage stamps by the Government of St. Kitts in 1990.

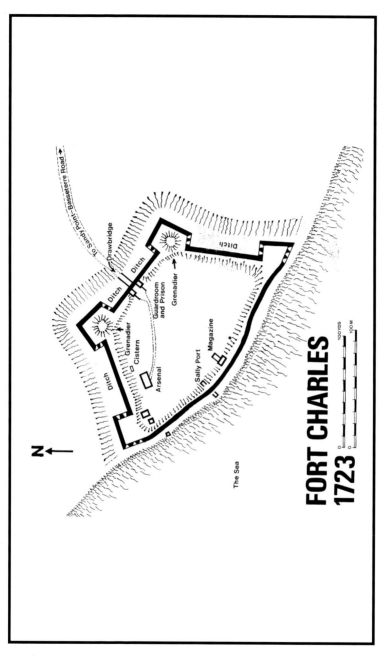

Plan of Fort Charles in 1723. Based on an original in the collection of the Duke of Buccleuch. V.T.C. Smith

This event led the English to view Brimstone Hill in a new light. Permanent gun positions were then placed on the Hill, both to deny a similar use being made of it by the French against the English in the future, and to support Fort Charles with artillery fire from the rear against the possibility of land assault. By 1699 Brimstone Hill had 18 cannon, probably mounted on field-type carriages. Reportedly, it had sufficient supplies to hold out against an enemy for six months. Already the value and use of the Hill was being seen as more than just a support to Fort Charles.

The Hill remained uncaptured when, in 1706, the French again invaded the English part of St. Kitts and took possession of the island for a short period, after which the whole of the territory passed into the effective control of the English - a control later confirmed and made internationally legal by the Treaty of Utrecht in 1713. During the invasion, some civilians had joined the military forces on Brimstone Hill for safety. This suggested to the English that the Hill should become a regular place of refuge in the event of further invasions of the island.

CHAPTER TWO

THE BUILDING OF A REFUGE FORTRESS

To create such a retreat, by the mid 1720s the defences of the Hill were greatly enlarged and made into a fortress under Lieutenant-General Mathew.

The works of the fortress were designed to achieve two main objectives: firstly, to defend against infantry attacks up the ravines and accessible slopes which led to the upper part of the Hill, which had to be kept secure as a retreat; and, secondly to give fire-support to Fort Charles from the rear, as well as to cover the adjacent anchorage of Sandy Point.

To defend against infiltration by infantry, stone bastions and ramparts were built to block access at the three most vulnerable places. These defences became known as the North West, North East and South East Works (1723 plan on next page). Artillery was mounted in these works, to fire on their near approaches and sweep the sides of the Hill. Artillery support to Fort Charles and the anchorage, was provided from specially-placed embrasures in the North West Work.

In addition, a small citadel known as the Mincepye on the northern of the twin peaks of the Hill had several positions facing the country to the north and the tiny Colonel Woodrop's Battery on the ridge of the south ravine did have some command of the country nearby. However, the fortress does not appear to have been designed to withstand a major siege.

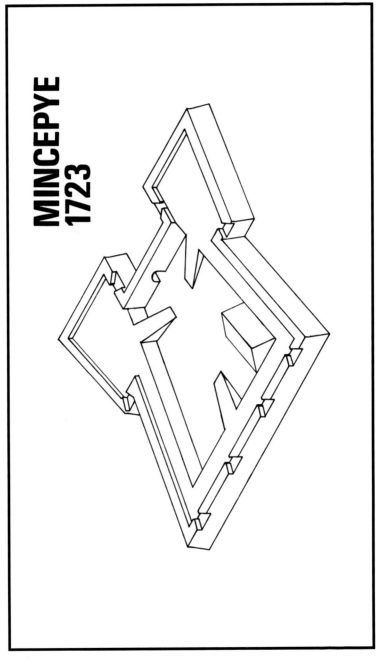

MINCEPYE 1723

Impression of the Mincepye in 1723.   *V.T.C. Smith • 1991*

16

Except for the Governor's House on the southern of the twin summits of the Hill, the only other buildings which seem to have existed within the fortress by the mid 1720s were a forge and two cisterns.

The fortress had just two entrances. The main one was at the top of the south ravine and was reached by a steeply graded road. The second entrance was at the north of the fortress, reached by an even more steep and narrow track.

By this date, the defences had, in the words of an official British document, become such "...as would defy any attempts of the French to dis-possess us, which they are liable to do whenever they shall incline to, or receive positive orders from France". Since at least as early as 1721 the free inhabitants of St. Kitts had been allowed to build houses on the Hill in time of peace so as to have existing habitations to which to retreat in war. Such "Refuge" fortresses were not unusual on the islands of the Caribbean. The neighbouring island of Nevis had one at least as early as 1699.

Construction of the Refuge Fortress continued into the 1730s. This involved great difficulties and tremendous feats of engineering. Although the fortress was largely adapted to the ground, huge amounts of rock and soil had to be moved in order to achieve the required results. Money for the work was difficult to obtain. Without the labour of slaves, released to work on the project, hardly anything would have been accomplished.

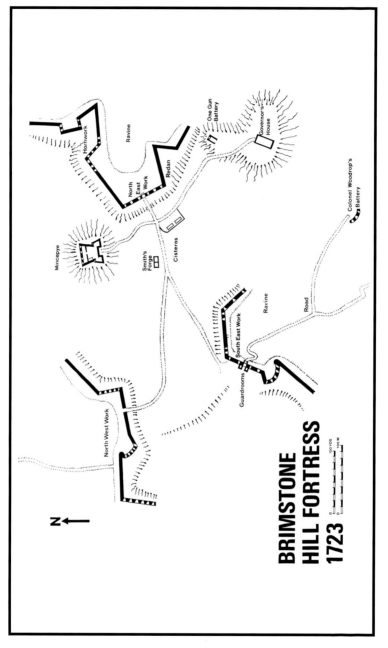

A plan of the Brimstone Hill Fortress in 1723. Based on an original in the collection of the Duke of Buccleuch.   V.T.C.S.

18

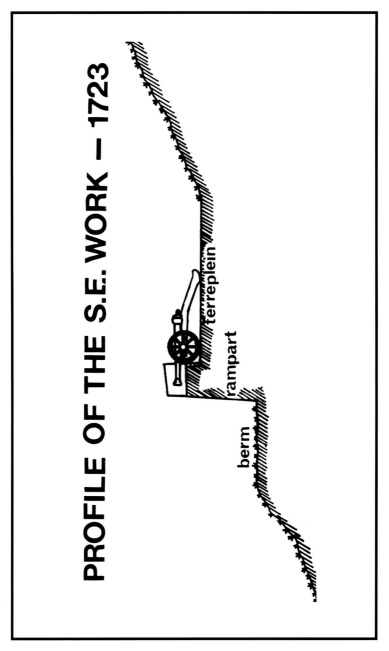

PROFILE OF THE S.E. WORK — 1723

terreplein

rampart

berm

Profile of the SE Work at Brimstone Hill, showing the type of ordnance mounted in 1723.   V.T.C. Smith • 1991

By 1734, the fortress had 63 cannon, from a tiny 1-pounder to an 18-pounder but few weapons that could be said to be suitable for effective counter-bombardment fire in the event of a siege.

As the defences became more organised, so further internal buildings were added, such as a capacious magazine (probably in the North West Work) and a 150 ft. long bomb-proof barrack (possibly the building later used as an Ordnance Storehouse in the South East Work). Two more barracks were to be built to "shelter women and children in case of bombardment". By 1753, the fortress had achieved an armament of 70 cannon and mortars, with over 4,000 rounds of ammunition and a large quantity of hand grenades to throw down into the ravines against enemy attempts at infiltration.

The walls of this early phase of the development of the fortress are traceable in the coursing of their irregularly shaped stone blocks.

CHAPTER THREE

THE GREAT SIEGE OF 1782

In 1782, the fortress was besieged by an overwhelming French force and Brimstone Hill again echoed to the sound of gun-fire. During the month-long battle the fortress was not a good place to be as its walls, structures and the upper slopes of the Hill were blasted by shot and shell, sometimes both by day and night.

France had allied with the Revolutionary government of the American colonies in 1778 and French naval and military operations against British interests in the Caribbean ensued. By the time St. Kitts was invaded by 8,000 French troops in January, 1782, a number of British islands had fallen. Indeed, it began to seem as though the end of the British territorial presence in the Caribbean was in sight.

In fact, the invasion of St. Kitts came as no surprise, for an attack had been expected for well over a year. During 1781 some new gun positions had been established on the landward side of the fortress, new magazines and cisterns built and thorn-hedge obstacles established in the more vulnerable areas. However, the fortress remained ill-prepared to resist a regular siege and retained a number of defects in design, with its parapets in a decayed state.

When the French invasion force arrived, conveyed in 29 warships under the command of Admiral de Grasse, nearly 1,000 British troops took up position within the fortress.

These included parts of the 1st or Royal Scots and 15th East Yorkshire Regiments, island militia, detachments of the Royal Artillery and Engineers, together with a party of Royal Navy Sailors. The fortress was under the command of Generals Fraser and Shirley.

The fortress was soon sealed off from outside help by the French and was held in an ever-tightening grip. The French commander, General, the Marquis de Bouille, besieged the fortress in the usual European manner. This involved gradually encircling the Hill with artillery batteries, establishing supply parks and forming camps of large bodies of troops in case of sorties by the garrison or attempts by the British to relieve the fortress. The loss of a French supply ship, which ran aground off Sandy Point at the start of the siege, was just a temporary set-back for de Bouille.

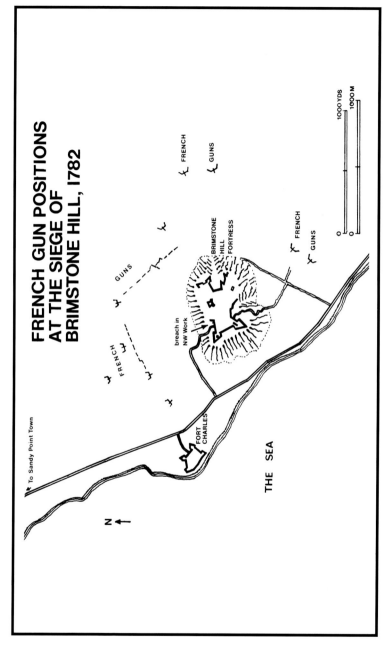

French gun positions at the siege of Brimstone Hill in 1782.
Plan by Victor T.C. Smith • 1990

23

On 24th January, the British Admiral Hood was successful in enticing the French fleet out of Basseterre Bay, (9 miles to the east) where it had been moored and which he then occupied with his own warships. A military force under General Prescott was landed at Basseterre but was soon beaten back by the French army. Hood could not expose his ships to attack by the French fleet by trying to land a force at Sandy Point to relieve the Brimstone Hill Fortress. In any event, the British ships carried too few troops to decide the outcome of the battle on land. Without relief from the outside or re-supply, the fortress became doomed.

At the outset, the guns of Brimstone Hill were able to fire upon and discomfort the first artillery positions established by the French. However, the siege gradually developed into a battle of attrition between the two sides. The French were able to emplace increasing numbers of cannon, howitzers and mortars and to concentrate their deadly fire upon the fortress. The guns of the garrison had to disperse their fire upon a growing number of siege batteries and were becoming reduced in numbers because of disablements. Ammunition and other supplies were running out and could not be renewed.

As shot and shell rained down on the fortress, almost all the buildings became damaged or destroyed and the men of the garrison had to find shelter on the blasted surface of the Hill as best they could. With the power of their concentrated artillery fire, the French were able to cut two large breaches into the rampart of the North West Work, as a preparation for a general assault upon the fortress by their infantry.

The British garrison had no tools with which to build a second line of defence further back. After a month, just a few cannon capable of being fired remained in the fortress. These could neither compete with the large number of siege batteries nor prevent a close assault. Reduced in numbers by injury, sickness and some desertions, without sufficient weapons left to fight, or supplies to subsist, further resistance by the garrison became futile.

On 12th February, the garrison surrendered after a heroic resistance of over a month. De Bouille allowed the garrison the honour of marching out with flags flying and drums beating as a mark of his respect. Hood's fleet slipped away from St. Kitts on the day of surrender, following news that a large number of additional French warships were about to join de Grasse.

The action in St. Kitts had a wide strategic effect. The detention of so many French troops on the island and of de Grasse's fleet, prevented the French and the Spanish combining to invade Jamaica. With the past loss of so many other British Caribbean islands to the French, the capture of Jamaica might have meant the end of the British colonial presence in the West Indies. As it turned out, the time bought in St. Kitts led the way for the Battle of the Saints, off Dominica on 12th April 1782, during which a large French naval force was decisively beaten by a British fleet. British primacy in the Caribbean was thus re-established.

CHAPTER FOUR

THE "GOLDEN AGE" OF THE BRIMSTONE HILL FORTRESS

St. Kitts was returned by the French to Britain under the terms of the Treaty of Versailles in 1783. It is not known how much work was undertaken by the French during their tenancy of the fortress to repair its walls but they appear to have had plans to do so, had they stayed on.

When the British resumed control of St. Kitts, a scheme was devised not just to repair the damaged structures of the fortress but to try to learn from the deficiencies of past planning and to design an improved layout of defences. This re-design had, as its object, the construction of a fortress sufficiently strong to resist and survive a regular siege and powerful enough to defend the Sandy Point anchorage at long range.

Under this scheme, the fortress was not only symbolic of British title to St. Kitts but provided a garrison of infantry, both as a security against the possibility of a rebellion by slaves on the island and as a reserve to be deployed, if needed, to join any British military expeditions mounted in the Caribbean.

The extensive and expensive programme of re-modelling which ensued from the mid-1780s was to lead to the Golden Age of the Brimstone Hill Fortress, when it became known as the "Gibraltar of the West Indies." It gave us the magnificent fortress which the visitor enjoys today.

Brimstone Hill Fortress.   *HMS Invincible • 1986*

To counter a bombardment by long-range breaching batteries, prepared emplacements were provided on new sites within the walls to fire upon those places on which an enemy might be expected to place his guns in a future siege. Knowledge of the places chosen by the French during the siege of 1782, appears to have been heavily drawn upon in planning.

The new high-sited defences were the Prince of Wales Bastion, the citadel known as Fort George, with its two outworks, and the emplacements on a mound called Monkey Hill (the southern summit of Brimstone Hill), with its outlying gun casemate. Other gun positions were provided in the older bastioned lines, which were repaired and in some places raised in height.

The defence of Fort Charles from the rear and of the Sandy Point anchorage was provided by guns mounted to overlook these places, both in the West Place of Arms and in the right face of the Prince of Wales Bastion.

The lowest level of the defences was the Barrier Redan. This guarded the road ascending the north of the Hill, which is now the main access to the fortress.

The armament of the fortress comprised more than seventy heavy, medium and light cannon, howitzers and mortars. These weapons were expected to fire up to 2-3000 yards, whether over land or sea. The cannon were initially mounted on ship-type wooden truck carriages, the howitzers on sturdy "field" carriages and the mortars on substantial beds.

Gun in the right flank of the Prince of Wales Bastion,
showing its command of slopes to North of Brimstone Hill.

Defence of the Hill slopes and ravines against infiltration remained important. Some of the near slopes could be covered by the cannon of the fortress but only firing at considerable angles of depression. The way into the fortress, via the ravines, was defended by short-barrelled Carronades and by small and light mortars. There were some areas of "dead" ground around the hillsides and special positions were formed so that they could be observed by the garrison.

Of the new defences, the most remarkable was Fort George, started in 1789 and substantially complete by the late 1790s. Described in contemporary documents as a "Beautiful Work", this is the earliest known surviving example in the British service of a radical new defensive system, called "Polygonal Fortification".

This rejected the bastioned fortification of earlier thinking. It substituted a more simple plan, with straight lines of rampart behind which was mounted the artillery to fire outwards. Close defence was provided by musketry fire from bomb-proof and loopholed vaults called "caponiers", which projected from the rampart walls into the ditch.

Fort George and its outworks viewed from the air.
HMS Invincible • 1986

South caponier of Fort George.
Photo by Victor T.C. Smith • 1990

A consequence of the new defences and of the maintenance within the fortress of an infantry garrison was the building of a considerable amount of barrack accommodation. For officers of infantry, a long and imposing two-storey barrack, with its lower level formed into a colonnade, was constructed at the west side of the flattened area known as the Parade, between the twin summits of the Hill.

Nearby, a most imposing and handsome quarters for the officers of the Artillery was built. Engineer, medical and other officers were accommodated in buildings elsewhere in the fortress. Enlisted men lived within a capacious barrack at Fort George, in a large barrack within the North East Work and in other places where spaces for buildings could be found. There were, by the Napoleonic Wars, so many buildings that the fortress assumed the appearance of a small mountain top town. This is shown in a number of contemporary drawings and paintings.

There was accommodation within the fortress for about 800 troops. However, the buildings rarely seem to have been fully occupied. Usually the garrison did not rise above a few hundred, of which a proportion were normally unfit through illness or other infirmities.

Infantry in garrison were various British Line Regiments which served on the Hill for 1-3 years. From the mid-1790s, black troops of the West India Regiment were often also in garrison.

Guns on the ramparts of Fort George, with mountains in the background. Photo by Victor T.C. Smith • 1990

Gun and embrasure in the East Place of Arms, Fort George.
Photo by Victor T.C. Smith • 1990

CHAPTER FIVE

HOW THE FORTRESS HAD BEEN REBUILT

As in earlier years, the structures of the fortress were built from the grey andesite stone quarried from the Hill itself but cut into neat, square blocks. The limestone of the Hill was burnt to make mortar to join the stone blocks together and a circular limekiln still remains in the brush at the bottom of the Hill.

Some of the limestone dressing stones to be seen in the buildings of the fortress may also have been cut from the Hill but may equally have been imported. Bricks were certainly brought from Britain and may be seen incorporated into some of the buildings. Where timber was used in the original structures, this was either long-lasting greenheart, or pine.

The remodelled fortress was designed by the Royal Engineers (RE). These were a small specialist corps of officers who designed and superintended the building of a wide range of military works. During the busiest years of reconstruction from the late 1780s until the end of the 1790s, the RE officers at Brimstone Hill were successively Lt. Lees, Lt. Col. Hay, Capt. Kirstiman and Lt. Hartcup.

These officers lived in quarters on the rising ground in the rear of the Magazine Bastion, whose remains may still be seen. (An RE officer continued to form part of the garrison after the main phase of reconstruction of the fortress was over).

Some of the reconstruction works were undertaken by British military artificers. Generally though, hard manual labour was considered injurious to health for European troops in this tropical zone. The vast majority of building was carried out by plantation slaves and "Government Negroes", who lived on the Hill during the period of the works and had their own medical facilities.

Over a hundred such workers might be on the site during the busiest times. They included many skilled men such as stonemasons and carpenters as well as fetchers and carriers of building materials. The fortress, including the beauty of the cut stone in its walls, is very much a product of, and a tribute to, their skills and efforts.

CHAPTER SIX

LIFE AT THE FORTRESS

The fortress became a complete military community in which the soldiers of the garrison lived, worked and sometimes died. Families of some of the soldiers also lived on the Hill. Under Army regulations, six wives per hundred men were allowed. The men authorised to bring wives with them were drawn by lot. With 300-400 men usually in garrison, family members might have amounted to over 60, with children, and including the families of several civilian staff who were resident in the fortress.

The vast majority of soldiers had to seek female company as best they could. The small number of females in the form of wives and daughters, resident in a large, closed and overwhelmingly male community must have created some social problems. Current practice quartered wives in the barrack rooms with nothing but a hanging cloth between them and the rest of the soldiers for privacy. It is known, however, that in the 1790s a small amount of married quarters was provided, albeit in a number of decayed and condemned huts.

Boredom was a problem for the troops. Except for the cooler beginning and end of the day when outside musters and duties could be performed, they spent much of their time in barracks, out of the sun. For day after day, week after week, there was little for them to do, other than to gamble and get drunk. In the claustrophobic conditions of the barrack room, petty differences and irritations between men became exacerbated.

As Medical Officers reporting on conditions in the Caribbean remarked, pay allowed soldiers to buy sufficient rum to keep themselves in almost permanent intoxication if they wished to do so. If drunkenness impaired the ability of a soldier to muster or undertake guard duties, he was punished. Discipline in general could be severe. Minor misdemeanours could be punished with lashes from the Cat O' Nine Tails. More serious offences might be punished with several hundred lashes, administered in stages with wound-healing periods between them.

Sunday worship was mandatory for the garrison but there was rarely a resident Chaplain at the fortress. A local Cleric probably visited. Religion in the Army was less about saving souls and more about reinforcing a sense of discipline. By invoking the words of the Bible, it was hoped to use religion to persuade men against drunkenness, gambling and other evils which interfered with their military efficiency and good order.

Feeding the stomach was as important as feeding the mind. A typical ration for troops was bread and cocoa for breakfast, soup, beef and yams for lunch and cocoa or coffee in the evening. This soldiers' diet was officially considered to be nourishing.

Foodstuffs were either brought across the ocean from England in casks or purchased in the Caribbean. When brought across the ocean they could be quite old and sometimes bad by the time they arrived. If salt-beef were provided this added to the soldiers' thirst and materially increased their consumption of rum.

The diet was not calculated to foster a sound constitution and, at the time, St. Kitts - as other islands in the West Indies - was not a healthy place in which to live. Indeed, because of the prevalence of disease and the liability to ill-health in the region, a posting from Britain to the Caribbean was sometimes viewed by the soldier concerned as practically a death sentence.

The greatest scourges and fears were Yellow Fever and Malaria, which visited the garrison from time to time. Both were spread by bites from mosquitoes but because this was not known at the time, proper counter-measures could not be undertaken.

Typically in West Indian garrisons, the soldiers (and civilians) suffered persistent stomach and bowel complaints, eye infections and a range of unidentified 'fevers'. Medical officers blamed the impurities of the rum consumed by the troops for much of the illness suffered. An average of 15 percent of the garrison were sick at any one time. The death rate was 5 percent per year under usual circumstances but was much higher during times of epidemic.

The excavated marker stones of a grave at Brimstone Hill.

The garrison cemeteries were well dug-over, as the same ground was used and re-used on many occasions, with previous burials being cut through for the new. The cemeteries probably contain the remains of several hundred soldiers and some civilians. Among the grave-markers is a memorial to Elizabeth, wife of sergeant William White, mother of ten offspring, who died on 23 October, 1810, aged 29, and who shared her grave with four of her children.

Hospital accommodation and a doctor were provided for the men but the ward assistants were often quite unskilled in even the rudimentary health care methods of the day. Soldiers tended to get extra specially drunk when in hospital, in the belief that this would speed their recovery.

Officers had better accommodation and food than the men and tended to spend less time sick. Both suffered the hot, stuffy conditions in their quarters and, if living in a timber superstructure, a most unpleasant solar gain during the hottest times of the year. All, too, had to put up with the intrusion of poisonous centipedes and sometimes scorpions in their living spaces. Few viewed their enforced exile from England with much favour.

CHAPTER SEVEN

THE FRENCH ATTACKS OF 1805 AND 1806

On 8th March, 1805, St. Kitts was again invaded by the French, this time under General La Grange, whose military force was carried in a fleet of 12 warships. Basseterre and part of the island were briefly occupied but British title to the island was retained by their continued occupation of Brimstone Hill.

In 1806, the guns of the fortress fired in anger for the last time. In July of that year, a French naval force under Prince Jerome Buonaparte advanced against British shipping moored in the waters off Sandy Point and under the protection of Brimstone Hill. The guns of the fortress, firing at long range from positions designed in the post-1782 reconstruction for just such an event, drove off the French.

The official British report of the engagement, glowing in its compliments for the determination of the garrison to resist the attack, does not record a single hit upon any French warship. It is probable that the fire of the fortress guns was in itself a dissuader to the French who must have not wished to risk damage to their ships by pressing home their attack too closely.

CHAPTER EIGHT

THE LAST YEARS OF THE FORTRESS

The garrison of the fortress, as all British garrisons in the Caribbean, remained ever watchful throughout the Napoleonic wars. British success at the Battle of Trafalgar in 1805 had not destroyed the threat of French naval power. France continued on with her vigorous programme of warship construction and the possibility of further raids or invasions must have seemed real enough. The attacks on St. Kitts of 1805 and 1806 were recent memories and underlined the existence of that threat. The older type wooden gun carriages began to be replaced by longer-lasting cast iron carriages and the defences were maintained in a high state of readiness.

The success of Britain and her allies in the Napoleonic Wars also confirmed British primacy in the Eastern Caribbean. Subsequently, many of the British defences on the various islands gradually slipped into decay but the Brimstone Hill Fortress was actively maintained for some years more. The other coastal forts of St. Kitts, with the exception of Fort Charles, seem to have gone unmaintained.

Some new building within the Brimstone Hill Fortress did take place, including the construction of the Commissariat Store at Parade level. This was capable of holding supplies of foodstuffs to last 500 men for 3 months. Several destructive hurricanes visited St. Kitts in the 1820s, 30s and 40s. During one of these the upper storey of the Infantry Officers' Barracks was so badly damaged

44

as to require demolition and replacement with three smaller buildings.

By the 1840s, the days of the Brimstone Hill Fortress as an active defence fortress were coming to a close. Its role as a coastal defence position had diminished in value with the reduction in importance of the anchorage off Sandy Point for British shipping.

The wider strategic value of the fortress had also declined: Britain felt herself to be in a strong position within the Eastern Caribbean and no longer needed to maintain a miscellany of fortresses and batteries on all of the islands.

As part of a general review of the defence of British colonial possessions in the Caribbean in 1853, the garrisons of St. Kitts, Dominica, Grenada, St. Vincent and Tobago were ordered to be withdrawn.

The garrison of Brimstone Hill was transferred to Barbados from which it subsequently went on to serve in the Crimean War.

The sound of bugle calls and the barked commands of Sergeant Majors to their troops were heard no more on Brimstone Hill. The fortress gradually decayed and fell into disrepair.

The wooden buildings were sold at public auction, stonework was robbed for building materials for use elsewhere, cannon were dismounted for removal for scrap, and the site became overgrown and obscured by brush.

Around the end of the nineteenth century, the historical consciousness of the Government of St. Kitts was stirred and it began to make an allocation of money to maintain some of the buildings, to clear brush and to make the site more accessible to visitors.

From then on, in the ensuing decades of the twentieth century, emerged a veritable "time capsule": an entire fortress of the Eighteenth Century and Napoleonic Wars, unaltered by later development, forming the remains of a complete military community.

The current restoration and interpretation programme of the Brimstone Hill Society is designed to bring the fortress back to life in the eyes, minds, understanding and memories of the visitor.

The inner side of the gate at the Prince of Wales Bastion.
V.T.C. Smith

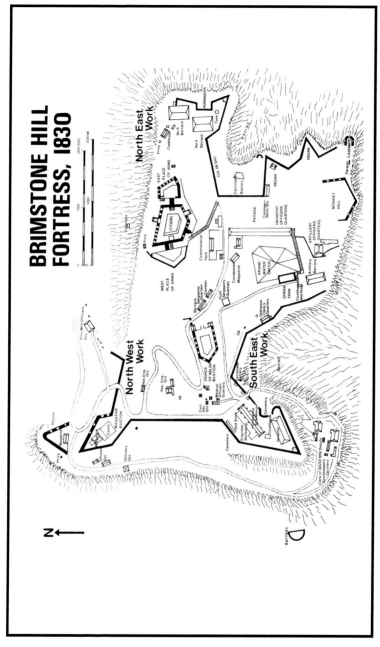

General plan of the Brimstone Hill Fortress in 1830.
Based on various plan evidence. Victor T.C. Smith • 1990

47

CHAPTER NINE

THE MAIN FEATURES OF THE FORTRESS
(Please refer to the the various plans for detail)

FORT GEORGE AND ITS OUTWORKS

This is the most prominent feature and the 'Jewel in the Crown' of the Brimstone Hill Fortress and was its citadel, built between 1789 and the late 1790s. It is reached by a staircase from the Parade. Fort George has two outworks known as Places of Arms on its eastern and western sides and is separated from them by ditches.

Fort George itself is in the form of an irregular pentagon. It is a very early example of an innovatory and new defensive style called Polygonal Fortification. In this, the key element is more efficient separation of long-range artillery fire from short-range fire for local defence than had been the case in the bastioned style of fortification. The upper rampart space was allocated for long-range artillery defence; local defence of the building was by musketry fire from within bomb-proof vaults called "caponiers" which projected from the wall. From the five "caponiers" of Fort George the whole of the front faces of the building could be defended with fire. The windows in the walls between the "caponiers" could also be used as fire positions for local defence.

The roof of Fort George has fifteen embrasures for cannon, firing north on potential enemy battery positions in a future siege, and to the south.

Above the west face is an observation platform associated with a now vanished signal mast nearby, and on the south face is a belfry.

The West Place of Arms was for seaward artillery fire and to cover Fort Charles; on its right flank is a half-casemated gun position facing north. The eight embrasures of the East Place of Arms look mainly to the land to the north-east of the fortress, again aligned on some likely sites for enemy batteries in a siege. Part of the fortress armament has been preserved and mounted in these places.

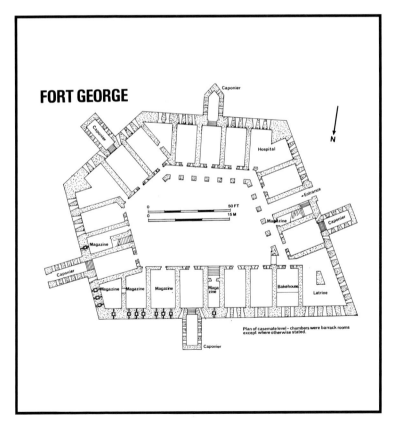

Ground Floor plan of Fort George. Victor T.C. Smith • 1990

Fort George itself is entered over a fixed bridge in its west face which gives on to an arch crowned by a plain triangular pediment. (A drawbridge, though intended, seems never to have been provided). Passing a staircase up to the roof gun positions, an entrance passage leads into the central courtyard surrounded by 23 bomb-proof rooms known as casemates, some of which are fronted by a colonnade. Fourteen of these rooms were for the accommodation of troops (who slept in hammocks), one each for a bakehouse, latrine and hospital and six in use as magazines. On the eastern side of the courtyard is a second flight of steps up to the roof of Fort George. Next to this, is a way through the East Caponier to the Eastern Place of Arms.

Rainwater which fell onto the roof of Fort George drained into a cistern within the building. A bomb-proof privy is on the edge of the space in front of the NW face of Fort George.

View of the interior of Fort George.
Photo by Victor T.C. Smith • 1990

50

MONKEY HILL

Across the Parade from Fort George, is the grassy mound of Monkey Hill, with its fine all-round views. It is ascended by a ramp which curves up to its summit, on which the Governor's House (no longer in existence) had been built by 1723. During the reconstruction of the fortress after the siege, it gained some artillery positions to fire on the ground to the south and south-east of the fortress, again places on which an enemy might locate breaching batteries in a siege. These works were started in 1793/4 with a view to building a self-contained fort on Monkey Hill but the project was never completed.

The remains of defence walls and five embrasures may be seen on the upper part of Monkey Hill. There is also a related and outlying blockhouse on the edge of a precipice about 50 yards east of this position. This is an enclosed casemate, with three gun-ports for short-barrelled weapons, known as Carronades. Some original soldiers' graffiti has been carved into the corner stones of the gun-ports.

THE PARADE
- including the Artillery & Infantry Officers' Quarters

The flat area known as the Parade, between Monkey Hill and Fort George, was used for the assembly and drilling of troops. This was an original feature of the fortress and is shown in a plan of 1723. At the south end of the Parade, at the base of Monkey Hill, are the walls of the Artillery Officers Quarters, which had been completed by 1791. There is also an adjacent cookhouse. The Artillery Officers' Quarters was the most handsome domestic building in the fortress. It was a two-storey rectangular masonry structure, with a pitched roof covered by shingles.

The ground floor of its south elevation was colonnaded, whilst the north elevation was colonnaded only at its centre. The surviving arches are in brick, covered in mortar plaster set upon limestone pillars. Next to the west elevation is a small tank, which would have been filled from run-off rainwater from the roof. Two artillery officers lived in this building. Nearby a flight of steps leads down to an open-fronted and arched privy, facing to seaward.

The impressive colonnaded basement remains of the Infantry Officers Quarters line the western edge of the Parade. Sometimes called the Grand Range, these quarters were built by 1791 to accommodate the officers of the infantry regiments who were more or less continuously in garrison. A dozen or more officers lived there. The normal living space was a vanished, mainly timber, building erected on top of the basement.

This building was so damaged in a hurricane of 1843 that it was replaced by three smaller structures on top of the ends and centre of the basement. These too have vanished but the one at the northern end has been replicated and is in use as a canteen for visitors to the fortress.

The colonnade of the Infantry Officers' Quarters.
Photo by Victor T.C. Smith • 1990

The basement is entered from a central staircase leading down from the Parade. It consists of a line of 13 casemates between a sunken passage along its Parade side and a second colonnaded walkway, which faces the sea. A central passage, from the bottom of the steps from the Parade, both divides the line of casemates into two and gives access to the colonnade passage. The doors to the casemates are off this passage. The semi-circular casemates were used as stores and, reportedly, one was used as a school room for children in the garrison. In wartime they would have been available for use as bomb-proof accommodation for troops.

THE COMMISSARIAT BUILDING AND YARD

Across the road from the north end of the Infantry Officers Quarters is the Commissariat or Supply Store and Storekeeper's Quarters with cookhouse, (later Warrant Officers Quarters). These are enclosed by a wall which formed the Commissariat Yard. These facilities date from about 1830 and were constructed close to the site of earlier buildings found in excavations in 1990. Food in barrels was transported by wagon up the Hill and into the store from a nearby supply depot on the shoreline. The Commissariat building and Storekeeper's Quarters were repaired and rebuilt in 1989/90. The Commissariat Store is now the Visitor Centre and the interiors of the Storekeeper's Quarters and of the adjacent Cookhouse are in the process of being restored to their original appearance.

On the slope above the western end of the Commissariat Yard are the remains of a privy of uncertain date.

THE NORTH EAST WORK

The eastern side of the Parade is bounded by a stone wall, which forms part of the North East Work. This special defensive position, which existed at least as early as 1723, was to protect the fortress from attack by enemy infantry coming up the East Ravine. The North East Work was designed to enclose the top of this ravine, which emerges on to a wide, flat artificial space, called a berm and, originally, into the field of fire of fourteen gun embrasures. The area thus formed was a kind of deadly cul-de-sac. It was formed of two curtain walls in a re-entering angle, joined on the left to a pair of bastions and on the right to a V-shaped angle (called a Redan) pointing to the country. A second Redan was added sometime before the Siege.

Barracks in the North East Work. Victor T.C. Smith • 1990

Visible on the outer face of the wall of the cul-de-sac are six blocked gun embrasures and a doorway which gave access to the berm from the parade. In the walls of the already-mentioned pair of bastions, which joined to the left of the cul-de-sac, are further blocked gun embrasures. Within the area enclosed by these bastions are the prominent ruinous walls of a large infantry barrack. It had a "furrow and trough" double-roof and a central brick-arched wall divided the building in two along its length, with a gallery along either side.

Next to this is the rectangular platform for a further barrack and, nearby, a cistern. The hexagonal pit close to the SE corner of this barrack was to receive a cast iron water tank. On the nearby point of the right-hand of the two bastions is a raised gun platform of Napoleonic date.

THE GRAND WATER CATCHMENT

The Grand Water Catchment, which may date from the early 1780s, is the enclosed downward slope on the seaward side of the Infantry Officers Quarters. It originally had a smooth cement surface which conveyed rainwater, which fell upon it, into three underground cisterns at its foot. The large and open cistern (known as the Green Tank), which is next to these, was filled by a separate rainwater channel from the Infantry Officers' Quarters. The Green Tank, is reached from a staircase down from the south end of the Infantry Officers' Quarters or from a trail up from the Orillon Bastion. The entrances to the three underground cisterns may be seen. Close to the wall of the Green Tank are the remains of a barrack for enlisted men of the Royal Artillery.

The Grand Water Catchment.   *Victor T.C. Smith • 1990*

A few yards to the north of the catchment is a vaulted structure known as the Condemned Magazine, which dates from the eighteenth century. It was probably condemned because, in its position, it was liable to flooding in heavy rain. Inside its entrance is a small lobby for handling gunpowder and filling shells and, behind that, the storage chamber for powder barrels.

THE PRINCE OF WALES BASTION

The Prince of Wales Bastion and its gateway, were completed by the middle 1790s. The bastion was designed as a powerful fire position, to command further ground that might be occupied by future besiegers. It also supported Fort Charles from the rear and was capable of firing out to sea.

The bastion consists of two faces and two flanks, pierced with embrasures for eleven guns. A prolongation to the rear of its right flank is a guard house, with underlying store, and the gateway itself which bears the date 1794 on its outside pediment. The prolongation to the left is a magazine, to which a modern lavatory was added at its rear in the 1970s. The original privy is at the foot of a flight of steps a few feet away from the recent addition. In the rear of the bastion is a ramp into its centre where, in 1810, a shed was built to contain an armament of mobile artillery to supplement the fixed guns of the rest of the fortress. The bastion has been re-armed with artillery.

Through the opening in the wall, across the road from outside the gate, was a place used as a small market for local people to sell to the garrison.

Prince of Wales Bastion (right) & Orillon Bastion (left).
Photo by Victor T.C. Smith • 1990

THE SOUTH EAST WORK
- AND THE ORILLON BASTION

The South East Work is of similar date and purpose to the North East Work. Its role was to enclose the top of the south ravine and to guard what had, until the siege, been the main access road and gateway to the fortress. It consists of the Orillon Bastion itself and the curtain wall (with gateway) extending from it east and south east.

Within the Orillon Bastion is the long building, which may have originated in the 1730s as a barracks. Five partially-blocked gun embrasures may be seen in the curved left flank of the bastion and several more along the curtain wall. The South East Work is the best part of the Brimstone Hill defences to see the appearance of the original fortress because it has been least altered by post-siege development.

The original gun positions of the South East Work were abandoned no later than the date of the siege. New positions, which can be seen, were built on the point of the Orillon Bastion and on its left flank.

After the siege, the Orillon Bastion also became a specialised part of the fortress. It became its Medical Centre, Ordnance Store and Repair Facility. The low rubble and turf mound behind the left face of the bastion is the foundation of the former garrison hospital. The medical officers lived on the slope just in the rear of the bastion, where the foundation terraces of their accommodation may still be seen.

West end of Ordnance Storehouse, showing the inner arch of original construction. *Victor T.C. Smith • 1990*

The long central building in the bastion became the Ordnance Storehouse for the fortress, in which all manner of equipment such as spare timber gun carriages and small arms for the garrison were kept.

The building originally had a semi-circular roof and thinner side walls. However, for some reason, the building split down the centre of its arch and the two side walls subsided.

To strengthen and retain the structure, the walls were doubled in thickness and a new pointed roof added over the arch, to give it the appearance which it presents today.

Along the south side of the storehouse is a rainwater cistern.

Behind the north side of the storehouse are the remains of the Engineer, the coopers' and the carpenters' workshops.

In front of the walls of the bastion were the two garrison cemeteries: one apparently for NCO's and their wives and children, in front, in the alcove of the flank of the bastion and this is marked by visible gravestones.

The other cemetery, apparently for enlisted men, was in front of the right of the bastion. The dead seem first to have been placed in a mortuary just inside the sally port (as the gateway had become) and then taken out for the burial service and interment.

Also, outside the walls, about 150 feet below the left face of the bastion, are the remains of the quarters for the Deputy Storekeeper and Clerk of Works.

Finally, there should be mentioned a small semicircular battery for three guns perched on the edge of a precipice about 200 feet below the right face of the bastion.

This had a field of fire to seawards. Its foundations are badly eroded and it is gradually collapsing over the edge.

Caponier on the south face of Fort George.   *V.T.C. Smith*

THE NORTH WEST WORK
- AND MAGAZINE BASTION

The curtain wall extending north from the right flank of the Orillon Bastion connects with the Magazine Bastion of the North West Work.

The bastion has two front faces making a point to seaward and two flanks. The curtain wall, extending east from its right flank, is pierced by a gateway and continues on to join with another flank wall which forms a revetment to the hillside behind.

The North West Work was the most heavily bombarded part of the fortress during the siege and was afterwards rebuilt in neat, square blockwork decorated with a cordon.

It was on almost the same plan as the pre-siege wall and the join line of the new with the old masonry may be seen in the left face of the Magazine Bastion.

Left face of Magazine Bastion, showing three phases of construction and repair - from the early 18th Century until the Napoleonic period.
Photo by Victor T.C. Smith • 1990

Two embrasures, in the right face, point outwards, towards some of the ground to the north which an enemy might occupy in a future siege.

A further two embrasures in the right flank both command a small part of the approach road up the Hill and the ground in front of the the curtain wall.

The gateway itself is surmounted by a plain classical pediment, containing the date MDCCXCIII (1793).

The Parade and Infantry Officers' Quarters, with Monkey Hill in the background and the restored Commissariat Store in the foreground.

The magazine that gave Magazine Bastion its name.
Victor T.C. Smith • 1990

The magazine which gives the Bastion its name, is a rectangular structure with a near parabolic outside roof section. It has a front Shifting Room for the handling of gunpowder and a rear storage chamber.

Its visible surface is in irregular blockwork and was present at the time of the siege. It may also have been damaged during the siege and subsequently repaired.

In the rear of the magazine is a rainwater catchment and a cistern.

The prominent stone walls of the quarters for the Royal Engineers and Mess Room, are terraced into the rising ground next to the road behind the Magazine Bastion. There may also be seen the remains of a staircase, several room layouts, a water tank and, in the rear, a roofed building.

The buildings on this site were originally of mainly timber construction but were later improved with a larger stone element.

In front of the left face of the Magazine Bastion is the site of the foundations of some officers quarters (previously temporary hospitals).

Reconstructed Warrant Officers' Quarters (circa 1830).

THE BARRIER REDAN AND GATE

The Barrier Redan and gate are to the front of the right face of the Magazine Bastion. A proposal in 1791, the Redan and gate certainly existed by 1799.

The salient of the Redan faces north and an extension of its right face is the gateway itself, which is the lowest gate of the fortress.

The right face of the Redan is pierced by three embrasures, whose guns commanded parts of the road approaches to the gate as well as some of the near hill slopes.

The left face of the Redan is simply a revetment to the ground in front but has a break through it to give access to a casemated privy.

In the rear of the Redan is a casemated building, the eastern part of which was a guardroom and the other end a small magazine chamber.

Originally, the Redan was fronted by a timber palisade against the possibility of a sudden onrush of troops.

APPENDIX

The Brimstone Hill Fortress is now the site of a National Park which comprises the 40 or so acres of Brimstone Hill. As such, the geology of this remarkable volcanic extrusion overlaid with limestone, as well as the flora and fauna it supports, are now officially protected and are being presented as additional attractions to the thousands of visitors - local and foreign - who come to St. Kitts each year to enjoy and to learn.

The Fortress, however, remains the principal attraction, and its presentation and interpretation are the major objectives of The Brimstone Hill Fortress National Park Society.

Long before 1965, when the forerunner Brimstone Hill Restoration Society was founded, the work of stabilization and restoration was begun. The late G. H. King I.S.O. was the moving spirit during this period.

The era of the Brimstone Hill Restoration Society, particularly during the stewardship of its President, Lloyd Matheson C.B.E., saw a more concentrated effort at restoration as well as a programme of reconstruction culminating with the Commissariat Building now adapted to use as the Visitor Centre.

During this period the Society was able to secure the services of a number of experts - notably Frederick C. Gjessing A.I.A., an architect with a special interest in historical restoration, and Victor Smith B.A., an historian with a special interest in British military fortifications.

Brimstone Hill Fortress National Park is the property of the Government of St. Christopher and Nevis, entrusted to our Society for its management and upkeep. The island's Government, including previous Administrations, has always been supportive of the Society's activities.

Financial assistance has also been obtained in the form of grants from individuals, corporations and external agencies, in particular, the Canadian High Commission and the British Development Division in the Caribbean, located in Barbados, to whom the Society wishes to express sincere gratitude.

The Society has now embarked on a programme of presentation and interpretation of the Fortress which, together with the ongoing work of restoration, will build on the legacy, not only of the designers and builders of this magnificent monument, but of the many who have laboured and assisted in retrieving it from ruin and vegetation and presenting it for the enjoyment and edification of present and future generations.

Brimstone Hill Fortress National Park Society